EARTH SCIENCE LIBRARY
MOUNTAINS
MARTYN BRAMWELL

Updated Edition

Franklin Watts
New York · Chicago · London · Toronto · Sydney

Second Edition
© 1987, 1994 by
Franklin Watts
All rights reserved

Franklin Watts
95 Madison Avenue
New York, NY 10016

Library of Congress
Cataloging-in-Publication Data
Bramwell, Martyn.
Mountains / by Martyn Bramwell. –
Rev. ed.
p. cm. – (Earth science library)
Includes index.
ISBN 0–531–14303–1
1. Mountains – Juvenile literature.
[1. Mountains.] I. Title. II. Series:
Bramwell, Martyn. Earth science
library.
GB512.B72 1994
551.4'32 — dc20   93–40313
                                   CIP   AC

Printed in Belgium

Designed by Ben White

Picture research by Mick
Alexander

Illustrations:
Chris Forsey
Colin Newman/Linden Artists

Photographs:
Ardea 1, 4r, 6, 10, 14r, 20, 23
Bruce Coleman 8
FAO photo 22t
GeoScience Features 9, 12br, 17r, 24l, 28
Robert Harding 14l, 21, 29t
Frank Lane 12tl, 14
Natural Science Photos 17l, 25, 27l
Planet Earth Pictures 13, 26
South American Pictures, 5, 19, 22b, 27r
Woodmansterne 29b
ZEFA 4l, 24r

EARTH SCIENCE LIBRARY
MOUNTAINS
MARTYN BRAMWELL

Contents

The roof of the world

Mountains provide some of the most spectacular scenery on earth. Some occur as single isolated peaks, but most form part of long mountain ranges or **chains** that run for hundreds of miles across the surface of the earth.

These towering barriers of rock are very important to us. Because they are so high, they affect the weather and climate over huge areas. They also control the flow of rivers. And because they affect the wind, temperature and water supply, they also control what crops can be grown in certain parts of the world.

Mountains are also very difficult to cross. In many areas they have prevented the spread of animals and plants from one area to another. The hummingbirds on the west side of the Andes, for example, are quite different from those found on the east side.

▽ A flowering rhododendron tree provides a surprising splash of color high in the mountains of Nepal. Rhododendrons are found throughout the Himalayas, in Japan, Southeast Asia, Europe and the United States. But of the 1,200 known species, more than 700 are concentrated in the eastern Himalayas.

△ Journeys that once took a week or more by foot and packhorse can now be made in a few hours on mountain highways.

People, too, have found mountains a problem. The Rocky Mountains were an obstacle to the settlers traveling west in their wagon trains.

For scientists, mountains provide a real treasure house of information. Biologists have discovered hundreds of rare plants and animals that are specially adapted to life at high altitudes. And by studying the rocks and structures of mountain ranges, geologists have discovered how enormous forces deep inside the earth have shaped our planet's surface over millions of years.

▽ Even in the highest mountains there are small areas of relatively flat ground with enough soil to allow crops to be grown. These Aymara Indian homes lie in the shadow of Mount Illimani, at 6,882 m (22,580 ft), in the Bolivian Andes.

Birth of a mountain range

About 100 years ago scientists first suggested that South America and Africa had once been joined together. Everyone agreed that their coastlines seemed to match very closely. But as nobody could explain how a huge continent could break up and drift apart, the idea was thrown out. Yet over the years more and more evidence has suggested that the continents had in fact moved about. But how?

The breakthrough came as recently as the 1960s in a new theory called **plate tectonics**. Geologists discovered that molten rock, called **magma**, was rising to the surface along cracks in mountain ranges deep beneath the oceans. As the new rock was forced upward, the ocean bed moved apart to make room. Far away, at the edges of the great oceans, just the opposite was happening. The moving slabs of seabed were being dragged down under the continents and destroyed.

▷ The Pacific seabed plate and South American plate are moving towards each other. Where they collide, the seabed is forced down as the continental plate rides over it. The collision zone is marked by a deep trough called an offshore trench.

Offshore trench

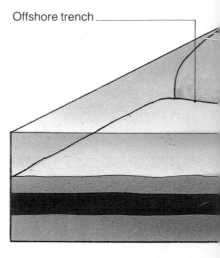

▷ The Paine Mountains lie in the southern part of the Andes – the great mountain chain that runs down the west side of South America. The range is 6,400 km (3,980 miles) long and contains the highest mountains in the **New World**. They include Cerro Aconcagua, Cotopaxi and the active volcano Antofalla.

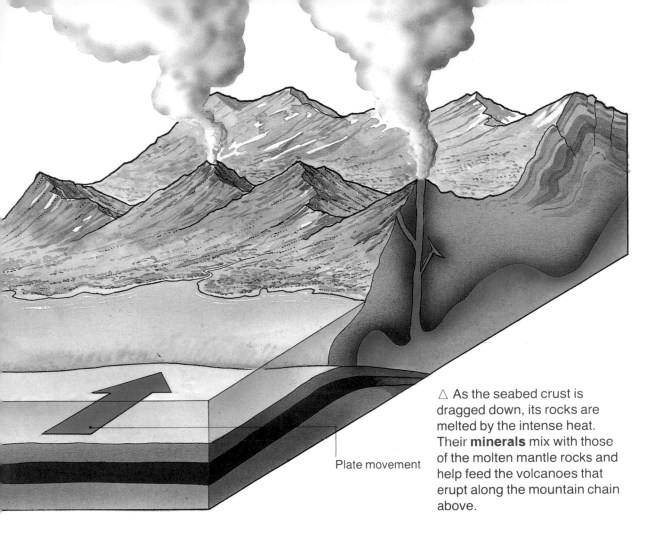

△ As the seabed crust is dragged down, its rocks are melted by the intense heat. Their **minerals** mix with those of the molten mantle rocks and help feed the volcanoes that erupt along the mountain chain above.

Plate movement

All these movements are driven by slowly churning currents in the **mantle**. This is a hot layer of partly molten rock. It lies just beneath the **crust** and the top, solid part of the mantle. The earth's outer layers are made up of about eight large "plates" and several smaller ones.

As well as answering the old questions about how continents could move, the new theory also explained how some kinds of mountains were made. Where the Pacific seabed plunges beneath the South American plate, the edge of the American plate is crumpled up into a mountain range. These "folded" mountains are made even higher by **volcanoes**, which build up their cone-shaped peaks from layers of **ash** and **lava**.

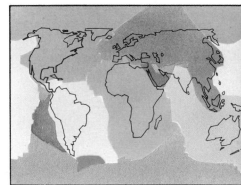

△ The earth's crust is made up of eight large plates and several smaller ones. New rock is added where the sea floor is spreading, beneath the sea. Old sea bed is destroyed at the oceans' edges.

Folding and faulting

Although we use expressions like "as hard as a rock" and "rock solid," the fact is that rocks can bend. They cannot bend quickly. Too much force will simply make them break. But if they are put under great pressure for a long period of time, they are slowly bent and pushed into **folds**, like wrinkles in a sheet or tablecloth.

Some types of rock fold more easily than others. Layers of **sedimentary** rocks like shale, sandstone and chalk fold quite easily. This is because some of the movement is taken up by the rock layers sliding over each other. You can demonstrate this with a pack of playing cards. Tap the edges of the pack on a table to make them smooth and square. Then hold one end very tightly and use the other hand to bend the pack. The tightly held end will remain square, but look carefully at the other end.

△ Folded layers of shale and limestone on the coast of Dorset, England.

▽ If you push a cloth into folds, the first small folds will stand fairly upright. But soon they roll right over like waves breaking. This also happens in solid rock.

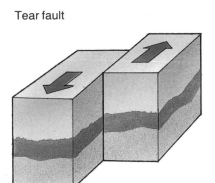

Tear fault

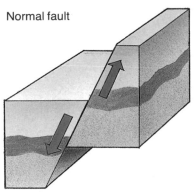

Normal fault

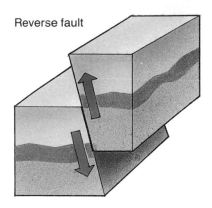

Reverse fault

△ Tear faults are formed where slabs of rock are being forced past each other. Normal faults occur where the crust is being pulled apart, reverse faults are formed where the rock layers are being crushed together by horizontal forces.

The cards will have slipped past each other, leaving the end of the pack looking like a series of tiny steps. If the cards had been glued together to prevent this slipping, you would not have been able to bend the pack at all.

Another important factor is heat. When rocks are squeezed by movements in the earth's crust, the deep rock layers become so hot that some of the minerals melt. They flow under the pressure and then cool and harden into new minerals. Geologists call the new rocks **metamorphic** rocks. The word means changed. They include many attractive building stones. Marble, for example, is limestone altered in this way.

However, if the pressure is too great or the movement too fast, the rocks cannot withstand the strain. They break at their weakest point. The break is called a **fault**.

Faults vary enormously in size – from tiny microscopic cracks in single crystals to massive splits in the earth's crust. The huge San Andreas fault runs for nearly 1,000 km (620 miles) through California.

△ In this photograph a group of geologists in Iran is examining a very steep (high-angle) reverse fault in sandstone beds. Compare the photograph with the diagram above. How far do you think the fault has moved the rocks?

The great collision

To understand how plate tectonics works, imagine a pot of jam simmering on a stove. Hot jam rises in some places and spreads out, carrying with it the froth and scum on the surface. In other places the jam sinks again, leaving the froth in small "rafts."

Something very similar happens inside the earth. Just below the thin hard outer crust is the mantle. It contains a layer that is kept partly molten by the intense heat inside the earth. Here currents rise, spread out and sink, carrying slabs of crust and upper mantle from place to place.

The currents are constantly changing, and sometimes two rafts will be pushed into each other so that they pile up into a thicker raft. That, on a gigantic scale, is how the Himalayan Mountains were formed.

About 200 million years ago South America, Africa, India, Australia, and Antarctica were all grouped together in one huge supercontinent. The great landmass then broke up, and the mantle currents carried the pieces far apart. As the Americas drifted westward, their edges were crumpled to form the Andes and the Rockies. India was carried farther and farther north until eventually it collided with Asia. Huge amounts of sand, mud, and silt had collected in the deep ocean basin between the two rafts. As these sediments were crushed, they were folded and bulldozed into a mountain range whose highest peaks rise almost 5.5 miles (9 km) into the sky.

The collision that created the world's greatest mountain range started about 65 million years ago. And it hasn't finished moving yet! The Himalayas are still rising.

200 million years ago

100 million years ago

65 million years ago

10 million years ago

△ By measuring the speed of plate movements today, geologists can "work backwards" and plot where the continents were millions of years in the past.

△ The magnificent peaks of the Mount Everest group in the Himalayas are 800 km (500 miles) from the sea. Yet here, on the roof of the world, are rocks that started out on the bed of an ancient ocean.

▽ The diagrams show three stages in the building of the Himalayas. As the "raft" of India approaches Asia, thick layers of sediments collect in the ocean basin between them. Slowly the ancient ocean is squeezed out of existence and its seabed rocks are crushed and forced upward. The main period of mountain building happened between 25 million years ago and about 12 million years ago.

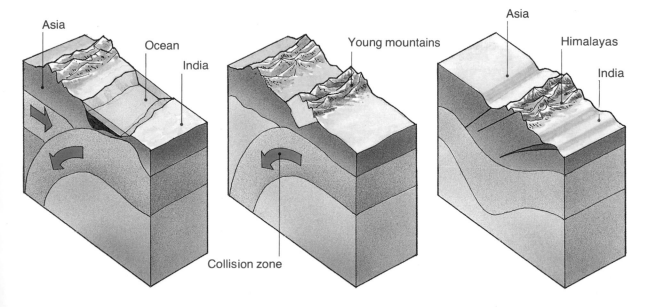

Most of the mountains we have looked at so far are quite young. The Alps, Himalayas, Andes, and Rockies are all roughly 60 to 70 million years old. The peaks are still high, and their ridges still sharp. But there are much older mountains, such as those of Scotland and Scandinavia, the Appalachians in North America, and the Urals in Russia. These ranges were pushed up more than 250 million years ago by an earlier set of mantle currents. The mountains are now much lower. Their shapes are softer and more rounded. Apart from some peaks in Scandinavia, few of them are more than 4,900 feet (1,500 m) high.

Further back still in the earth's history there were other mountain-building periods. But the mountains they created have long since vanished. What forces can break down and carry away an entire mountain range?

△ The Yellowstone River plunges over a 90-m (295-ft) fall as it carves its steep-sided valley through the mountains of Wyoming. The waterfall is caused by a band of hard rock in the river bed.

▷ Alternating bands of hard and soft rocks in the desert of Iran show the shattering effect of the desert climate. The rocks expand in the fierce daytime heat and then contract again at night. This causes them to crack and break up into pieces.

△ These strange natural sculptures are produced by a combination of flash floods and the blasting effect of wind-blown sand grains.

△ Water expands when it freezes. When water trickles into cracks in the rocks, and freezes at night, the force is enough to crack off fragments of rock.

The answer is surprisingly simple. As soon as a mass of land is pushed up above sea level it is attacked by wind, rain and moving ice, by temperature changes and by natural chemicals.

Some rocks, such as limestone, will dissolve in rainwater, but most **erosion**, or wearing away, is done by streams and rivers. They rush over the land surface, scraping away at it with the grit, pebbles and boulders they carry. In high mountains and other cold regions, rocks are broken down by ice and frost. The sharp rock fragments are carried away by **glaciers**, and these in turn gouge deep valleys out of the landscape.

In desert regions the temperature can vary from 50°C (122°F) at midday to well below freezing point at night. The constant heating and cooling makes the rocks crack and break up. But even in deserts, water is still very important. Rain may fall only rarely, but when it does it rushes over the dry landscape in **flash floods**. These sweep sand and stones downhill and carve deep gullies in the landscape.

Mountains on the move

△ A rock glacier in the Wrangell Mountains of Alaska. Rock glaciers are streams of rock fragments that move slowly downhill like true glaciers. The rocks are frozen together and they move partly by gravity and partly by alternate thawing and freezing of the ice that binds them together.

Breaking "solid" rock into small fragments is just the first stage in the erosion process. The next stage is **transportation**. The fragments are carried downhill until eventually they come to rest on lowland plains or are swept into the sea.

In deserts the main methods of transportation are by wind, and by the sudden floods when rain falls. In other regions rivers and glaciers pour down from the mountains carrying millions of tons of soil and rock. Large rivers carry huge amounts of debris – especially when they are in flood. Their waters turn brown with mud and even large boulders are swept along.

On steep mountain slopes, loose fragments of rock tumble down under the pull of gravity. And even when the surface is covered with soil, with the tangled roots of grasses and bushes to bind it together, the effect of gravity can still be seen.

On grassy hillsides the soil may creep slowly downhill, wrinkling the surface into gentle wave-like folds that sometimes make the slope look like a flight of stairs. And even when the soil is anchored by the interlocking roots of trees, a sudden downpour of rain or the jolt of an earth tremor can set the whole hillside in motion – with disastrous results.

△ This road in the hill country of Derbyshire, central England, was permanently closed after a landslide broke up a large section of road surface. The road had unfortunately been built on the site of a prehistoric landslide.

▷ Heavy rains probably triggered the landslide that left this huge scar on the side of a mountain valley in Papua New Guinea. Most of the debris has been carried away by the river, but the narrow valley is still partly dammed by fallen rocks.

15

Mountains and the weather

Mountains actually cover only a very small part of the earth's surface, yet their effect can be felt hundreds or even thousands of miles away. They have an important effect on climate, and especially on the amount of rainfall a region receives. The reason for this lies in the simple fact that winds are forced to rise up and over these natural barriers.

The air around us contains a certain amount of water. It is in the form of water vapor, which is invisible. The warmer the air is, the more water it can carry – up to a point. Once the air reaches this point, the excess vapor **condenses** into minute water droplets. These are so light they can drift in the air. We can see water in this form as cloud, mist and **fog**.

If a stream of warm moist air is cooled down, some of its water condenses. Fog and mist often form when moist air meets very cold ground for example. Air is also cooled when it is forced to rise. (Anyone who has been up a mountain will know how much colder the air is up there.)

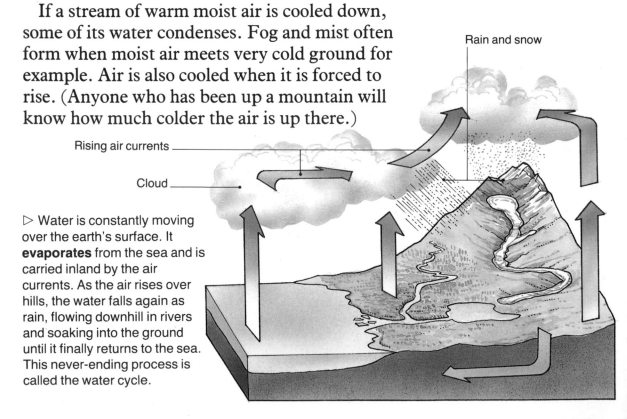

Rain and snow

Rising air currents

Cloud

▷ Water is constantly moving over the earth's surface. It **evaporates** from the sea and is carried inland by the air currents. As the air rises over hills, the water falls again as rain, flowing downhill in rivers and soaking into the ground until it finally returns to the sea. This never-ending process is called the water cycle.

As the air is forced higher, more and more of its water vapor condenses into cloud. The tiny droplets merge into larger and larger drops until eventually they start to fall as rain. The result is that the side of a mountain range facing into the main wind direction always gets much more rain than the "downwind" side.

By the time the airstream has crossed the mountains, it has lost most of its water. As it flows down the mountain slopes, it warms up very quickly. In some parts of the world these warm mountain winds have been given names. The chinook is one. It is a drying wind which sweeps across the northern plains after crossing the Rockies. Its name is an American Indian word meaning "snow eater." The föhn winds of the European Alps are very similar.

▽ The Cascade Range provides a perfect example of the "rain shadow" effect. Winds blowing in over the Pacific drop their moisture on the western slopes, which are clothed in dense, rich rainforest. Across the mountains in Wyoming and Montana the landscape is a mixture of dry grassland and scrub.

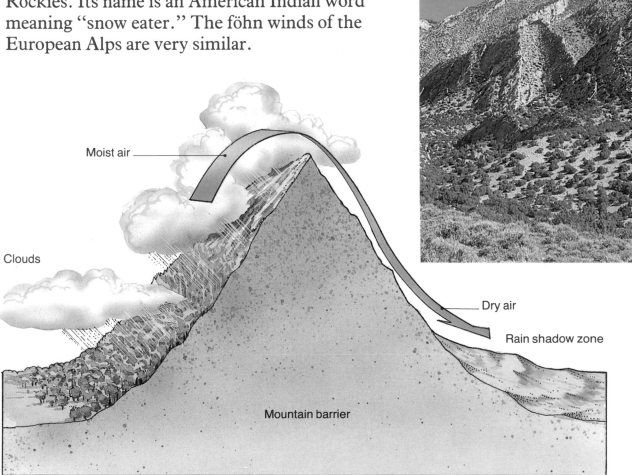

Moist air

Clouds

Dry air

Rain shadow zone

Mountain barrier

Who lives where?

The top of a mountain has much more in common with the distant polar regions than with the foothills and plains around its base. And the reason for this lies in the way that plant and animal life falls into distinct zones encircling the earth.

A journey from the equator to the North Pole would take you across a succession of different **habitats**. From dense tropical forest you would travel through **temperate** woodlands of oak, beech and maple, and then into dark **coniferous** forests of pine and fir. Beyond the forest you would emerge into a treeless world of frozen soils, covered in summer with mosses and lichens. This is the Arctic **tundra** – the last band of vegetation before the final wilderness of ice and rock.

▽ The main temperature zones that ring the earth have very similar counterparts in the living zones that are found on mountains.

Arctic
Temperate
Subtropical
Tropical
Tropical
Subtropical
Temperate
Antarctic

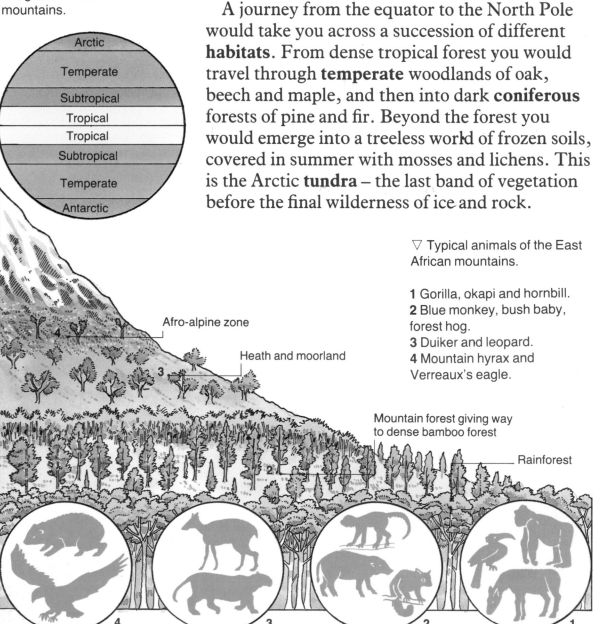

Afro-alpine zone

Heath and moorland

Mountain forest giving way to dense bamboo forest

Rainforest

▽ Typical animals of the East African mountains.

1 Gorilla, okapi and hornbill.
2 Blue monkey, bush baby, forest hog.
3 Duiker and leopard.
4 Mountain hyrax and Verreaux's eagle.

Almost identical living zones are found on mountains. Not all the zones will occur on every mountain, but the sequence is generally the same. Rich vegetation at the lower levels will give way to pine forests higher up. This will be followed by a zone of grassy alpine plants, the mountain equivalent of tundra, or other highly specialized types of vegetation. At the peak is bare rock, snow and ice.

Animals, too, are specialized for life at various levels in the mountains. Some keep to the woodlands of the foothills where food is varied and plentiful. Others have become adapted to live on the seeds of cone-bearing trees, or to hunt in the dark pine forests. Higher still are the alpine grazers, sure-footed and thickly furred, while high above the rock and ice zone the sky is patrolled by soaring eagles.

▽ Thin soils, low rainfall and low temperatures make farming difficult at this altitude in the alpine zone of the Peruvian Andes. The hillsides above the village support nothing but a layer of coarse grass. In the distance the bare slopes of El Misti, a dormant volcano, rise to a snow-capped peak at 5,840 m (19,160 ft).

The mountain specialists

Mountain regions provide some of our most breathtaking scenery, but for the animals and plants that live there conditions are extremely harsh. The air at high altitude is thin and cold. There is nearly always a chill wind blowing. Yet on still summer days the fierce heat of the sun can bake the soil as dry as dust and make the bare rocks unbearably hot. The soils themselves are thin and stony – very different from the deep fertile soils of the surrounding lowlands. Plants and animals alike share the problems of cold and wind, and the constant threat of drying out.

To survive in the mountains, trees and bushes have tough woody roots that can force their way into small cracks in the rocks to provide a firm anchor against the wind.

△ A Verreaux's eagle looks out from its cliff-top eyrie high in the mountains of Sudan.

▷ The ibex, a type of mountain goat, is one of the most sure-footed of all mountain animals.

▷ The puma, or mountain lion, is found in North and South America. It will eat almost any prey, from small mountain rodents to deer (its favorite food) and even domestic cattle.

△ Ptarmigan, blue hares and alpine marmots are all likely to fall prey to the majestic eagle as it soars high above a mountain valley in the European Alps.

But at the highest levels there are no trees. Here, the plant life consists of tough grasses and low, dense, cushion-like flowering plants. By keeping low, they avoid the danger of being knocked down by the wind. Their thread-like roots spread everywhere, turning the soil into an almost solid mat. The leaves of the mountain plants are usually thick and fleshy, and many are covered with fine downy hairs. Both are special adaptations that help cut down the loss of water on hot dry days.

Animals too need special "equipment" to live in the mountain world. Nearly all have thick shaggy coats to protect them from the cold. Compare the coats of yaks and llamas, mountain goats and mountain bears with those of their lowland relatives. Mountain sheep and goats are remarkably sure-footed and agile. Some even have rubbery pads on their feet to improve their grip.

To avoid predators, some animals like the ptarmigan, a plump highland bird, change their color to white in the winter. Other small animals, like the alpine marmot, retreat into deep burrows and **hibernate** throughout the cold winter months.

21

People of the mountains

◁ A Nepalese woman feeds her buffalo on leaves gathered from bushes. In some parts of the Himalayas so much of the forest has been cut down that village women may spend the entire day collecting enough fodder for their animals.

▽ Men from Bolivian mountain villages often find work in neighboring countries because of their ability to work at high altitudes. This Bolivian miner is working in the world's highest mine – a sulfur mine at 6,000 m (19,700 ft) on the volcano Aucanquilcha in Chile.

Living at very high altitudes can be a problem for people. The higher you go, the thinner the air becomes and the less oxygen it contains. That is why people who are used to living near sea level often feel dizzy and short of breath if they climb much above about 3,000 m (9,850 ft). And yet in the Himalayas and Andes and other high ranges there are towns and cities much higher than this. La Paz, the capital of Bolivia, stands at 3,600 m (11,800 ft). The Chinese town of Wenchuan on the northern side of the Himalayas is even higher at 5,100 m (16,750 ft).

The difference between lowland people and hill people lies in the red blood cells that carry oxygen around the body.

Mountain-dwellers have a much richer supply of red blood cells and this boosts the amount of oxygen they can take in from the thin air. Their bodies have adjusted to the special conditions of life in high places.

People from low altitudes can acclimatize to a certain extent. Athletes competing in high altitude cities, for example, arrive early. Over a period of a week or two their bodies will manufacture extra red cells. Climbers, too, will train in high mountain country before tackling a particularly high peak. However, the highest peaks of all are usually climbed with the aid of oxygen masks.

Life in high mountains is difficult for plants and animals too. The thin soils produce only small amounts of food, and very often the steep hillsides must be terraced before any crops can be grown. Livestock are a very important source of meat and milk and wool – especially yaks and buffalo in the Himalayas, and llamas and alpacas in the Andes. Cattle, hill sheep and goats are kept in many other mountain regions.

△ A flock of llamas grazing on coarse grasses high in the Andes of Chile. Llamas, alpacas and vicunas are members of the camel family. They are the only New World relatives of the humped camels of Asia and Africa.

Using the mountains

Mountain people all over the world have shown great ingenuity in the way they use the land. The building of terraces goes back many thousands of years. It involves an enormous amount of labor, but once terraced, a hillside can be used to grow rice, corn, vegetables and even fruit trees. The terraces not only provide flat growing areas, but their retaining walls protect the thin soils, preventing them from being washed away in the rainy seasons. They also help to hold back water which would otherwise drain away.

In the Himalayan valleys and foothills the main crops are rice, wheat, corn and millet. In higher regions, above 3,500 m (11,500 ft), tougher crops like barley and root vegetables are more common.

▽ Many of the world's largest copper mines are in mountain areas. The major producers include Chile, the United States, Canada, parts of the former USSR, Zaire and Zambia. This photograph shows the huge open-cut mine at Mount Morgan, in East Queensland, Australia.

△ These remarkable rice terraces in the Philippines have turned almost the whole of the steep valley sides into productive farmland. And they have been in continuous use now for more than 2,000 years.

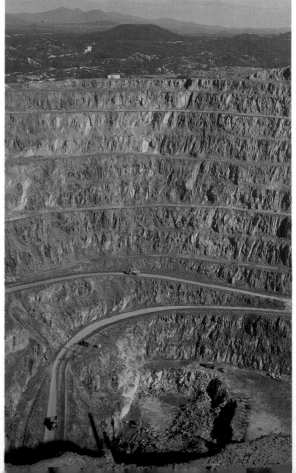

In the highlands of the Andes, potatoes are one of the main crops, along with maize and wheat and barley. And there, on the vast windswept **puna** – the 4,000-m (13,000-ft) high plateau in the mountains of southern Peru and Bolivia – large flocks of llamas, alpacas, vicunas and sheep are tended for their valuable wool.

In many parts of Southeast Asia the hills are still covered in dense forest. The people there live in small groups, hunting forest animals, gathering fruits and wild honey, and using a farming method called "slash and burn." The group will clear a patch of forest by cutting and burning and then plant corn, taro and sweet potato crops. When the soil is exhausted, usually after a couple of seasons, the group simply moves on and clears another patch of forest.

▽ An aerial view of small-scale cultivation in the forests of East Borneo. In the foreground crops are growing on recently cleared land. Near the top of the picture, older patches are being taken over again by forest. But hardly any of the original forest remains untouched.

The fragile giants

Fragile is not a word normally used to describe a mountain. But it is a very accurate description of the mountain habitat. The great hill forests that once covered most of the world's mountains are fast disappearing. And the tragedy is that of all natural habitats, these are among the most difficult to repair.

Most of the damage is caused by people, who cut down the forests for many different reasons. In some areas the forests are cut for their valuable timber. In other areas they are felled to make way for crops, or for herds of cattle, or even for buildings. In the highlands of Nepal entire hillsides have been stripped bare of vegetation.

▽ Forestry is a major industry in many hill regions. Most of the developing countries depend on the export of timber to earn money with which to buy food.

Here the local people are often forced to cut into the remaining patches of forest because they are desperate for fodder for their animals and for firewood to heat their homes and cook their food. Even the shifting cultivators are now damaging the forests. There are just too many people using the forests in this way. In some areas the forests are simply not given time to recover before they are cut down again.

The result of clearing the mountain forests is disastrous. Robbed of the protective layer of trees, the thin soils are washed away by the first heavy rains. The hillsides are left bare. And down in the lowlands, reservoirs and **irrigation** channels are clogged with silt and rivers overflow their banks, ruining huge areas of valuable farmland.

▽ The inevitable result. If the hillsides are not replanted, erosion takes over completely. Forest scientists have calculated that the amount of soil washed into the sea each year from the mountain slopes of Java would provide enough farmland to feed 15 million people.

△ A bare hillside in northern Thailand. The trees have been cut so that their valuable timbers can be exported to the richer nations of the world.

Serving the cities

△ A reservoir in the hill country of Luzon in the Philippines. The huge lake was created by building a concrete dam across a narrow mountain valley.

The millions of people who live in lowland valleys and plains still have many links with the distant mountains. Rivers that rise in the hills carry drinking water to small towns and villages. They provide water for irrigation and a natural drainage system for farmland. Many larger towns and cities take their water supplies from lakes in the mountains or from reservoirs created by building dams across mountain river valleys.

The amount of water used by city dwellers is enormous. While many poor countries manage on less than a gallon of water a day for each person, average water use in the United States is more than 100 gallons a day..

Industry too needs its water supply – often in surprisingly large quantities. More than 45,000 gallons of water are used in making a ton of steel.

Electrical power for many towns and cities comes from **hydroelectric** stations in the hills. Water from natural or artificial lakes flows through tunnels or pipelines and into the huge turbines that drive the generators. Although the costs of building the dam and power plant are high, the generators are very efficient and last longer than coal- or oil-fired power stations.

Hydroelectric projects have many benefits, especially in developing countries. As well as providing electrical power for new industries, they can be designed to help control flooding and to provide water storage for large-scale irrigation programs.

Mountain regions also provide an important means of relaxation. People flock to the hills to walk, climb and ski. Perhaps most important of all they offer a way of simply getting away from the rush of city life.

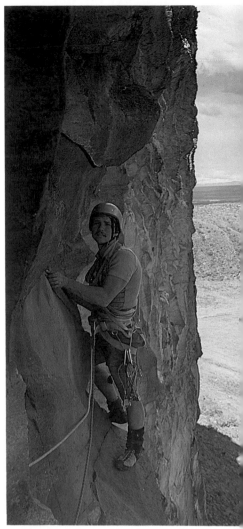

△ For those who take their leisure seriously, the mountain world provides some of the toughest challenges of all. Here a rock climber explores a new route on a sheer rock wall at Hell's Gate near Naivasha in Kenya.

◁ Vacationers pack the ski slopes of Europe and America every year. Winter sports form an important part of the tourist industry in many mountain regions.

Glossary

Ash Very fine droplets of lava blown out of an erupting volcano. When the ash hardens, it turns into a rock called tuff.

Chain A mountain system consisting of several ranges lying parallel to each other. There may be areas of flat land between the ranges. If these are at high altitudes, they are called plateaus.

Chinook A warm dry wind that blows across North America from the Rockies. It can raise the temperature by 30°C (86°F) in less than an hour, which is why the Indians named it the "snow eater." The wind can sometimes cause problems if it arrives too early in the spring. Plants start budding and animals shed their winter coats – a serious problem if there is another very cold spell.

Condense To change from a gas or vapor into liquid. Clouds are formed when water vapor condenses from the air.

Coniferous Means "bearing cones." Coniferous forests are evergreen forests of pine, fir, spruce etc.

Crust The hard outer layer of the earth. The stony crust is about 6 km (3¾ miles) thick beneath the oceans but averages 35 km (22 miles) thick under continents. Beneath mountain ranges the crust may be up to 70 km (43 miles) thick.

Erosion The wearing down of the land surface by water, ice and other natural forces.

Evaporate To change from liquid to gas or vapor. It is the exact opposite of condense. After a swim you can dry off in the sun because the heat evaporates the water off your body.

Fault

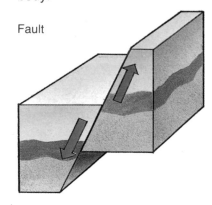

Fault A break in layers of rock caused by movements in the earth's crust. The break can be caused by a sideways tearing movement, or by stretching forces or by crushing forces.

Flash flood A sudden and violent flood caused by heavy rain characteristic of desert regions. The water cannot soak into the hard-baked ground, so it rushes over the surface, often causing severe erosion.

Fog Clouds of tiny water droplets floating in the air close to ground level. Fog is simply cloud that forms very low down in the atmosphere.

Föhn winds Warm winds that blow down valleys in the Alps. They are very like the American chinook wind. Föhn winds can be very dangerous. They can start avalanches, and in Switzerland can make the forests very dry – so increasing the danger of fires.

Fold A bent layer of rock caused by sideways pressure. Fold mountains are formed when plates collide. The Himalayas and Alps were formed in this way.

Glacier A moving river of ice that flows down a mountain under its own weight. Glaciers carve their own valleys, much deeper and wider than river valleys.

Habitat A word used to describe where an animal or plant lives. Forest, tundra, river bed and grassland are all different kinds of habitat.

Hibernation The process of passing the winter in a kind of deep sleep. The animal builds up its reserves of fat, then sleeps in a sheltered nest or burrow and its body processes slow right down.

Hydroelectricity Electrical energy generated by using the force of moving water in a river or flowing from a natural or man-made lake.

Irrigation The process of watering farmland by means of

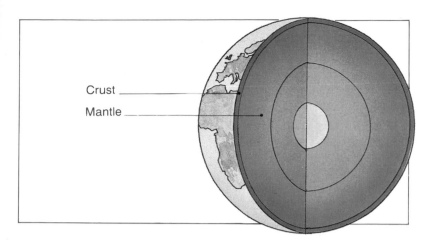

Crust

Mantle

Temperate The word means moderate, and is used to describe the climate zone between the warm tropics and the very cold polar regions. Most of Europe, the United States and Asia lie in the north temperate zone.

Transportation The movement of sand, soil, dust and other debris from one part of the earth's surface to another.

Tundra The barren area of frozen land lying between the northern forests and the snowfields of the Arctic regions.

Volcano A mountain or hill, usually roughly conical in shape, through which lava, gases, vapor and volcanic ash erupt on to the earth's surface.

channels dug in the ground or by sprinklers and other devices.

Lava Molten rock that pours out on to the earth's surface when a volcano erupts.

Magma The molten rock of the mantle layer, directly beneath the crust of the earth. Magma becomes lava when it reaches the surface.

Mantle The thick layer of semi-molten rock that lies beneath the crust. Movements in the mantle cause the crustal plates to move over the earth's surface.

Metamorphic A word used to describe rocks that have been altered by heat and pressure. Marble is metamorphosed limestone: slate is altered clay or shale.

Minerals The chemical building blocks from which all the different rock types are made. Quartz is the most common mineral. It is made up of silicon and oxygen. The tiny

glassy grains in a handful of beach sand are worn-down fragments of quartz.

New World A name often used to describe North and South America. The Old World refers to Europe, Asia and Africa.

Plate tectonics The name given to the theory that the Earth's crust is made up of moving sections or plates. It explains how the continents have moved and how certain mountain ranges have been built up.

Puna The high plateau that lies between ranges of mountains in the Andes of Peru and Bolivia. It is a high treeless tableland, very flat and windswept, lying 4,000 m (13,000 ft) above sea level.

Sedimentary The word used to describe rocks that started off as loose fragments sinking to the bed of a lake, river or ocean. They include sandstone, mudstone, chalk and many others.

Volcano

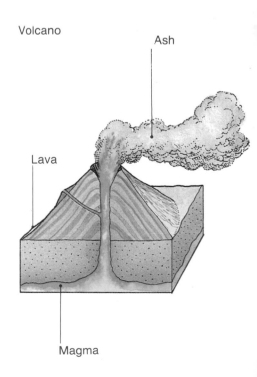

Ash

Lava

Magma

Index

PRINTED IN BELGIUM BY
proost
INTERNATIONAL BOOK PRODUCTION